Driving For Dur

Dedication:

For you, Christine, my daughter's old college roommate,
Something you said has stuck with me clear to this date:
"Her day's schedule in the paper she should publish,
Then drivers in her way justly earn her anguish."

Likewise, I realize, justified I am not,
Holding drivers to rules that they were never taught.
So, hoping they improve, or rage to justify,
Some good driving manners to instruct I will try.

©
Copyright Pending

Driving For Dummies

Introduction

The smart or robot car seems to be on the way,
It seems certain our roads they will control some day;
And our human error that they will then replace,
So our many mistakes hopefully they'll erase.

Automated drivers, while definitely new,
Probably may not be better than me or you;
But they're being the same removes uncertainty,
Correcting mistakes made from our diversity.

Because if all of you, drove just the way I do,
Or perhaps all of us, drove just like one of you
(Well, except for a few, that we will later name),
Then traffic would be fixed, if we're driving the same.

But driving all the same is not our better suit,
Different ways and rates all of us tend to scoot;
There's enough bad drivers I wouldn't trust too far,
It's sure OK with me, bring on the robot car.

But, since self-driving cars are still some years ahead,
And I'd still just as soon not wind up being dead,
Here's a refresher course on successful driving,
Some good simple guidelines for all our surviving.

I'll try for light-hearted, maybe sometimes funny,
Entertaining enough, so it's worth the money;
But still underlying, I hope to educate,
There's so much to traffic that laws don't regulate.

Driving For Dummies

Objective: The Flow

The basic elements of driving we all learn,
At home or Drivers' Ed when our license we earn.
My concerns are the things that effect traffic flow,
So, on the road we all get where we want to go.

A commercial back when, had this cute happy scene,
With things all working together so nice and clean;
Until some oddball tries differently to pay,
And chaos then results, 'cause he went his own way.

With hundreds, thousands, millions out there on the road,
We sure need to find a cooperative mode;
It's not at all far-fetched, that many of us think,
The roads would be safer if we're all more in sync.

Now the old traffic laws are good for what they do,
They do give some guidelines we pay attention to;
But as we're all driving weapons of destruction,
There are unwritten rules worth further instruction.

As we're driving along we should rightly expect
Consistency, unless a warning we detect;
Any sudden changes in direction or rate,
Are things we'd like to hope you would communicate.

Indeed, we're asking for some common courtesy,
On the rest of us poor souls please show some mercy;
If you would interrupt our normal traffic flow,
At least, for goodness sake, then please let us all know.

With an ample warning of your upcoming change,
Our own driving patterns we can then rearrange;
Then on your driving skill we're not forced to depend,
With opportunity, ourselves we can defend.

Now, of course, this implies that you really do care,
And others on the road you are at least aware;
Not off in your own world, and just oblivious,
Unawareness makes it hard to be courteous.

With a two-ton weapon moving at any speed,
Those of us around you hope that you will pay heed;
For that brief moment the road together we share,
We would sure like to hope you are at least aware.

So this lesson attempts some ideas to impart,
To make the traffic flow smoothly, more like an art.
An overall message in these thoughts to instruct:
Whatever that you do; please, please, please don't obstruct.

Driving For Dummies

Characters

For this simple lesson to really make some sense,
And also to not put the reader on defense,
We need some characters, that could be anyone,
To make as examples, and we can poke some fun.

They're drivers we've all seen, man, woman, girl or boy,
And though not all the same, each of us they annoy.
No matter the gender, they could be any age,
With their way of driving, they can drive us to rage.

The names we will give them, sex and age may imply,
But to be specific, we sure don't mean to try;
While the names we're giving for this lesson will do,
They could be anyone; shucks, even me or you.

Ploddin' Paul

The long line of traffic is barely at a crawl,
And of course in the front is good old <u>Ploddin' Paul</u>.
With the steering wheel gripped and his jaw tightly set,
He doesn't give a darn if in your way he'll get.

By golly he has to get from here to o'er there,
And anybody else on the road he don't care.
He's driving at the speed that he knows is just right,
And the whole world be damned, he won't vary the slight.

He knows he has a turn five or ten blocks further,
So this lane Paul will clog, no way he will detour.
Flash your lights, honk your horn, it falls on his deaf ear,
He doesn't even know that you're anywhere near.

Chatty Patty

The light has turned to green, but here she still does set,
Totally unaware, she's working on a text;
Swerving between the lanes, crossing the line badly,
Give her plenty of room, it's our Chatty Patty.

She's got so many friends with whom to text or talk,
She has no time to check where you might drive or walk;
Her path you should avoid, you shouldn't interrupt,
Sure don't want to distract the next thought to erupt.

She doesn't have a clue where other cars are at,
But that missing detail doesn't bother our Pat;
Apparently others should be watching for her,
It's all up to us should an accident occur.

Nervous Nell

She creeps out on the road, so very, very slow,
As she's apt to get hit, she's hesitant to go;
So, slowly she starts out, with fears she can't quite quell,
Oh please, cold cruel world, look out for Nervous Nell.

They are braking up there, nearly half mile ahead,
So Nell slows down some more, to catch up she would dread.
Her turn is coming up, a block or two or three,
She'll slow down to change lanes long before she can see.

Up the highway ramp, like a dog on his belly,
Creeping slowly along, it's our good old Nellie;
She just knows at the top there will be a big mess,
That she will be the cause, she can't begin to guess.

Zippin' Zack

Here he comes, there he goes; he is here, now he's there;
Always in a hurry, never seeming to care;
Darting from lane to lane, he is on the attack,
Look out everyone else, here comes that <u>Zippin' Zack</u>.

Like a video game, there is no consequence,
He'll never have a wreck or cause some accidents;
The world is his own stage, and it's all about him,
He's apt to make a pass on just the slightest whim.

Don't bother good old Zack with your worry or doubt;
If other dumb drivers the roads would be without,
Everything would be fine, he could get where he wants,
And there'd be none to scowl at his silly, dumb stunts.

Now we have some to use, some drivers to refer,
We could use some others, there are plenty for sure;
For there is no shortage of bad drivers out there,
It seems like we spot them just about anywhere.

For other's shortcomings are easy to detect,
But if we pause a bit and ourselves we inspect,
Interestingly enough, at some point in time,
Most all of us have been guilty of each one's crime.

Driving For Dummies

Lanes

Like hundreds or thousands of ships passing at night,
And all of them going at a high speed of flight,
Yet passing within feet, maybe inches apart;
Driving out on our roads is not for faint of heart.

But still, there we all are, cruising along our way,
So they've given us lanes, in which we should all stay;
'Cause it'd be dangerous, and just darn right silly,
To all go our own ways, driving willy-nilly.

We prefer to avoid making any contact,
Because at any speed, bad things come from impact;
Maintaining correct lanes is one way to avoid,
Contact or narrow miss, that leaves us all annoyed.

Like inertia, a natural law which to heed:
One's entitled to an established lane and speed.
Once we're rolling along, should be just to expect,
That our right to continue others will respect.

So we hope that others show consideration,
Their minds are not off on extended vacation;
They carefully maintain the lane they occupy,
And they think through it twice before changes they try.

First and foremost in making a lane selection,
Please make certain it is going your direction.
Whatever is the speed, if you're not the right way,
Going against traffic will sure mess up your day.

In the wrong direction it's not safe to enter,
So here in the U.S. we stay right of center.

"Wrong Way" "Do Not Enter" are not just some advice,
To not pay attention, the results won't be nice.

A drive you need to make, you have some place to go,
Along with the traffic, you find you need to flow;
First thing to remember, to make it there OK,
Again, please be certain, you're going the right way.

So now you're on the road, with traffic you're cruising,
And you want to change lanes, and not get a bruising;
Let's do a few quick things, before you start to veer,
To not endanger you, or anyone else near.

When we make lane changes for whatever reason,
Then, suddenly, we become "open season."
As staying in one's lane is rightly expected,
Our ventures out should be carefully directed.

There is some difference between town or highway,
But the rules still apply pretty much the same way.
Sometimes the lanes may be separated in two,
But sometimes they're just marked and crossing's up to you.

A median or wall we all know not to cross,
But a solid line also a barrier does cause,
And crossing over it makes you the one to blame,
If someone is there and into their path you came.

The first step to lane change, then, is making darn sure,
That it's even allowed, wherever you prefer;
Even if no barrier, you must see far enough,
To make the change complete before things get too rough.

Then the next step should be to make sure you have room,

Midst all the neighbors zipping by, going zoom;
Before you slide over into that spot you've seen,
Make sure there's enough space so you can make it clean.

Like was said before, drivers are justified,
To maintain space and speed at levels they've arrived;
So the change between lanes that you now plan to make,
Should not force anyone, to speed up or to brake.

It's the one changing lanes that may need to adjust,
To flow with the traffic that is always a must,
Whether to slow down some, to not crowd one in front,
Or speed up so someone doesn't slow to a grunt.

You've found your spot and you know to slow or to speed,
But there's still one more thing that you also do need;
Before the change you start, please turn your signal on,
Hopefully long before across the line you've gone.

The signal's whole purpose is to communicate,
It doesn't do much good if it's given too late;
Give us some fore-warning, this change you plan to do,
Then when you make your move, we can watch out for you.

Neither is it OK, to signal far ahead,
Where it confuses or your intent is misread;
You've been blinking for blocks, on you we've given up,
Then you make your change and traffic still will disrupt.

If well executed lane changes are harmless,
Everybody's happy, no delays and no mess;
Nobody is upset, 'cause nothing has gone wrong,
And traffic is still flowing happily along.

Here about now a good example we could use,
So some of our characters we're going to choose;
We will let them show us how it can be done wrong,
And all we have to do is just follow along.

So we have Zippin' Zack cruising in the left lane,
Talking to his best friend about a girl named Jane.
Meanwhile, Chatty Patty is over on the right,
Texting her friends about a guy she met last night.

Suddenly, good old Pat comes upon Ploddin' Paul,
She's right on top of him in just no time at all.
With a quick look she swerves and to her left she goes,
Signaling as she does, for what good no one knows.

Probably by this time, you have a darn good hunch,
There'll be those screeching tires and nasty metal crunch;
But let's say Zack makes it, he get's slowed down today,
He's pissed and flips her off as he drives on away.

With some more attention Pat could have recognized,
The need for a lane change as it materialized;
She could have slowed down some, let old Zack zip on by,
Turn her signal on, and around Paul she could fly.

Makes no diff'rence to Paul, he's still moseying on,
But a lot better Pat's and Zack's days would have gone;
They'd both still be visiting, rather than complaining,
The bad driver they saw, to their friends explaining.

About lane selection, there's some more to be said,
Another basic rule, we should get in our head:
"Slower traffic stay right," I'm sure you've seen this sign,
And now it's importance, I want to underline.

For whatever reason, which there are quite a few,
We go different rates in all the things we do;
Some like to go faster, always in a hurry,
While others are slower, not a care or worry.

Now there are speed limits, but that section's later,
And for those good comments, you must be a waiter;
Still, with the speed posted, it is not at all strange,
The rates being driven cover quite a broad range.

Our purpose here is not to argue wrong or right,
In the section on speed, we'll pick up that old fight;
But the different rates, we need to recognize,
So each goes their own way, with no hurt or demise.

The basic rule, at which we all need to be deft,
Slower traffic stay right, let the faster go left.
Once again this just helps, the traffic to let flow,
So everyone gets wherever they want to go.

So doing the limit, are you the slow or fast?
Doesn't really matter, if you're still getting passed.
It's a relative thing, what are others doing,
Are you being pursued or are you pursuing?

All things being equal, no one else is around,
The answer is simple and not all that profound;
Coming up on someone, to the left you should go,
If someone is catching you, staying right, let's them flow.

Now that's simple enough, no big news created,
Add more cars on the road, gets more complicated.
With everyone going at their own comfort rate,
It seems on each other we often have to wait.

Here's where we can help out, use cooperation,
And move us all along with much less frustration.

Using another lane you find you have to do,
We'll let you borrow it, but hurry and get through.

You're in your right lane and someone's slower still,
Passing in the left lane, it is certain you will.
Lane change rules do apply, and speed you should adjust,
Fit in for the moment, please don't abuse our trust.

It is not all that hard, other cars' speed to judge,
So please make note of it, before you start to budge;
An opening comes up that you decide to use,
Then please speed up enough, momentum we don't lose.

And now you are out there, your pass you start to make,
Forever and ever, we ask that you don't take;
Nothing much can be worse than two cars side by side,
Half the world caught behind, held up by their slow stride.

The left lane you borrowed, so let's get the job done,
And give it back to those who faster choose to run;
Show us this small respect, the favor we'll return,
On those occasions that into your lane we turn.

Left-turner in the way, a right turn to be made,
There are some times we find to the right we must wade;
The rules work in reverse, we should adjust our speed,
For our slower neighbors we also must pay heed.

Back to our characters once again we will turn,
Another example for us all to discern;
Let's let our brand new friends that we've just met today,
Show us all what happens when it's done the wrong way.

Our dear, sweet Nervous Nell is caught behind Ploddin' Paul,
She's been trailing awhile getting nowhere at all;

A meeting she must make, it's still a long way there,
And scary as it seems, a pass she plans to dare.

Lots of cars have gone by, a big gap she now has,
She turns her signal on and slowly starts to pass;
Zippin' Zack was way back, but it doesn't take long,
He is right behind her thinking this is so wrong.

Paul is locked at forty, Nell's doing forty-two,
It will be a long time before this pass is through.
Slowly, oh so slowly, Nell edges up along-side,
Both she and old Paul are white-knuckled and glass-eyed.

Now Zack is in a fit, he can't believe his luck,
While Nell is still gauging, if back right she can tuck,
Through the widening gap impatiently he zips,
A rant on drivers' age he furiously rips.

But there just dead ahead, Chatty Patty cruises,
In some conversation, 'bout boyfriends she loses;
Zack accelerates more to squeeze back left of her,
And he thinks to himself, "how good am I, for sure."

Once again, each of them roll along their own way,
Thinking screwy drivers are on the road today;
Others' imperfections, always easy to see,
Yet all equally glad, "there's nothing wrong with me."

Driving For Dummies

Speed

When we're out on the road and we're going somewhere,
Driving among others on roads we have to share,
There are six possible directions to watch out,
To check for and avoid any dangers about.

There are both of our sides, on our left or the right,
Then there is to the front, and the back, out of sight;
But then there is also surrounding you and I,
A top and bottom to the space we occupy.

Top or bottom, that is, from above or below,
There isn't much danger, from anything we know;
There's still no flying cars out there buzzing around,
That at the wrong moment could suddenly come down.

Proper lane etiquette will protect on each side,
That topic is discussed somewhere else in this guide.
Now to the front and back the dangers we should heed,
Pretty much all of these are the result of speed.

The speed we are going, whether it's fast or slow,
Determines what we meet as on our way we go;
What we come upon or what comes upon us,
As much as anything, the speed we're driving does.

Now it's true, we all know, speed limits are the law,
But how we all comply, presents a little flaw;
As it seems no matter what number's on the sign,
What it means to us we differently define.

Some of us always want to be right on the nose,
No faster or slower that person ever goes;

Like there's some penalty, if one's not just exact,
And somewhere driving points they're going to subtract.

Then there are timid souls, who think you must not touch,
That speed limit at all or you'll blow up or such;
Better stay some under, so that there is no risk
Of getting stopped and then away to jail they'll whisk.

Some drivers think they have got it all figured out,
That there's some tolerance, some benefit of doubt;
You can go over some, but keep it safe enough,
Police are so busy, they won't take notice of.

Of course, there are those, who simply just don't care,
Signs don't apply to them, and they speed everywhere;
They think they'll be lucky while police are off guard,
And so the silly signs they simply disregard.

Now, who is in the right, and who's terribly wrong?
And, who of all these types on our roads don't belong?
Again, it matters not, in spite how strong you feel,
As they are all out there, with them we have to deal.

The ones that always speed, are a problem, of course,
But that's a police job, speed limits to enforce.
And we don't even know, what's their situation,
Could be emergency has caused this occasion.

It could be life or death in a hospital run,
Rather than our first guess, some people having fun;
The point is we don't know, probably never will,
Our concern is just how it tests our driving skill.

Again it's relative, what's going on around,
Fitting in the picture, in which ourselves we've found;

No matter the limit, the traffic will dictate,
The right speed we should go, the appropriate rate.

If the traffic is light, not many on the road,
No need to worry, just pick your favorite mode;
At your comfort level you can just simply cruise,
Doing whatever speed that you decide to choose.

You may still have to deal with the authorities,
If you break any laws in their territories;
We might stare and chuckle, but there will be no fuss,
We don't care as long as you're not bothering us.

Let them enforce the laws, with traffic we're concerned,
Healthy interaction is what we hope is learned;
When traffic gets busy, we're sharing space and time,
That's when speeding mistakes become a social crime.

By now some may think that the solution I claim,
Is to all be alike, we should all drive the same;
As I said back before, that a robot can do,
But I'm pretty darn sure it won't work for me and you.

We all drive different, and that is still O.K.,
But driving together, we have to figure out a way,
To safely interact so that the roads we share,
Take us where we want with minimum wear and tear.

The important first step to figure proper speed,
The traffic around us to be aware and heed;
"What the traffic will bear" is often how it's said,
How others are driving must be constantly read.

Knowing how fast or slow our neighbors are going,
Helps us set our speed as through traffic we're flowing;
Avoiding getting bogged, or not causing a bog,
Not letting us get clogged, or not being the clog.

Monitoring others we pick the proper rate,
There are times to hurry and there are times to wait;
If we do a good job in these choices we make,
A lot less precious time our own journey will take.

In the section on lanes, attention was given,
How on the right the slower cars should be driven;
If the faster traffic to the left can get by,
Traffic will flow smoother, including you and I.

Traffic patterns do change as we all roll along,
And who's going faster may change before too long;
Often we should adjust either our lane or speed,
If others around us we notice and pay heed.

Waiting for a moment before left we do veer,
To get around the car we came upon it's rear,
So someone who's faster can go ahead around,
Great driving etiquette in this can sure be found.

Speeding up to get by so we can move back to the right,
Let's the car behind us continue his smooth flight;
Maybe the speed limit we exceed for a bit,
'Twill be that other guy, if someone they do git.

That helpful cruise control lots of us like to use,
To keep us just about the speed we like to choose;
But it gets annoying, some of us might confide,
If forced to kick it off when someone's broke our stride.

Now it is easier to speed up and fall back,
Then to have to slow down, then resume our attack;
One might keep that in mind as we're out there cruising,
And not mess others up, their momentum losing.

Let's say I'm passing you and to the right you are,
But you're coming upon a somewhat slower car;

If I speed up a bit and hurry on past you,
You can move left to pass without slowing down too.

Now in Washington State, there's a law that they post,
Six vehicles trailing, legally is the most;
So, at whatever speed, it's a violation,
To not pull over and ease the situation.

Making such adjustments may avoid a problem,
So it's helping us all, it's not just helping them;
The less interruption, the smoother traffic flows,
The quicker and faster everybody goes.

Getting somewhere quickly, is not just going fast,
If you get stuck in jams that it's hard to get past;
All working together traffic snags to avoid,
Moves us all along and keeps us all less annoyed.

So let's check on our friends, they're all out there today,
Using the interstate and just driving away;
With all different plans, still suddenly somehow,
They've all came together in the same place just now.

Chatty Patty is in the left lane just cruising,
Consoling a good friend whose boyfriend she's losing;
While she has no idea, she's right on the limit,
And cars are stacking up behind her quite a bit.

Now Ploddin' Paul is set smack dab in the middle,
Which way he'll need to turn is still a big riddle;
His speed locked at fifty, no way he'll ever change,
Everyone else will just have to rearrange.

Meanwhile, good old Nellie is coming up the ramp,
There's a line behind her, those who there had to camp;
About ready to merge, she's almost at the top,
Scared that there'll be no room, she's almost at a stop.

In the left lane comes Zack, he's been zippin' along,
When suddenly there's Pat and her unhappy throng;
Zack zips to the right and suddenly right there,
The end of Paul's long line is looming in his glare.

Zipping right once again, he'd hate to hit the brake,
Just as Nell gets her nerve and her big chance does take;
Now braking and skidding, Zack pulls up a hair short
Of creaming Nervous Nell, though he should he'd report.

Zack squeals off to the left with cursing and gestures,
There's lots of mad drivers, to old Nell it assures;
Zack whips back around Nell, and then accelerates,
They shouldn't be allowed, he very loudly states.

Catching up and cutting back right in front of Paul,
Hoping to make sure that he noticed his close call;
And then the same with Pat, Zack cuts in front of her,
After all, she's the cause and she should know for sure.

Pat does pause some in her lengthy conversation,
At least long enough to express indignation;
Meanwhile, our good old Paul just keeps plodding along,
Wondering what makes others drive so doggone wrong.

Zack doesn't realize it would have been faster,
If he would have slowed some to help getting past her;
Slow down to get past Paul, then move into that lane,
Pass Pat on the right and no one's shorts would they stain.

Of course, Pat should notice traffic she did obstruct,
After getting past Paul to the right could have tucked;
Letting the faster traffic on the left get by,
And never missed her friend's sad comment or a cry.

And poor Nervous Nellie, we wish that she would know,
To merge into traffic, their speed you have to go;

And while it is true that it takes a little trust,
At least that much confidence is surely a must.

As for Paul, probably we're asking too darn much,
To pay attention to other traffic and such;
Still if he would at least stay over on the right,
There'd be more room to pass without causing a fright.

So, once again we see if together they'd try,
They could all get along and make the traffic fly;
None of them would get stuck, and soon enough they could,
Resume their normal speed, once flowing like they should.

So what is the right speed? What is the proper rate?
To the circumstances that answer must relate.
While many rates are fine, the ones we don't instruct,
Are if others you endanger or you obstruct.

Driving For Dummies

Turns

Another obstruction happens in traffic flow,
When diff'rent direction we decide we must go;
To the left or the right we need to make a turn,
Again, there are some rules that we all need to learn.

Almost always a turn means we have to slow down,
And it takes some effort to not make others frown;
Turns take extra time and others may interrupt,
Making them unhappy when their flow we disrupt.

Proper execution our turn can expedite,
So we're less annoyance than otherwise we might;
And less interruption, as before we have said,
Keeps the traffic flowing, reducing all our dread.

Just as noted before we have to start with care,
Of others around us at least being aware;
What traffic is doing, if we make sure we know,
Our turn we can get made and some courtesy show.

Though sometimes a surprise, mostly well in advance,
We know our turn's coming, there's time for making plans;
And by planning ahead our turn we can complete,
With the least disruption or disturbance to meet.

Having been driving in the appropriate lane,
Elsewhere herein we did previously explain;
We've made a proper change to be in position,
So we'll be ready to turn the right direction.

Now, sometimes they provide a turn lane we can use,
Which is a great feature we hope you won't abuse;
Their goal is getting the turner out of the way,
So behind the turner traffic won't have to stay.

Getting in the turn lane as quickly as you can,
Traffic moves along and you don't get overran;
Don't think about it and dilly-dally awhile,
While stuck behind you the traffic begins to pile.

When you're in a turn lane you need to close up space,
If distance between cars you can try to erase,
More turners will fit in, less risk of sticking out,
Obstructing traffic, defeating what they're about.

Whether into a turn lane or making a turn,
To obtain the new direction for which you yearn,
Your speed you'll most likely need to downward adjust,
A change in our pattern which you suddenly thrust.

Those of us around you think we're just to expect,
A signal or some kind of sign to that effect;
Some communication, change is 'bout to occur,
So we too can slow down or better yet detour.

As is discussed elsewhere, timing of a signal,
Is important and can be equally crucial;
Make sure it's soon enough that others can respond,
But not run forever, where we've forgot and yawned.

A turn correctly made, should stay in the same lane,
From right into the right, the turner should remain,
And left into the left, if they're going that way;
Properly make the turn and in that lane should stay.

For if you cross-over, as so often we do,
You make it hard for us, as we try to miss you;
There will be time for a proper lane change to make,
A little further on and less risk will it take.

How fast to make a turn with circumstance varies,
On the car's driver and what cargo it carries;
But on present traffic it should also depend,
Behind you forever none of us want to spend.

Now, we're not suggesting you go so fast to turn,
That your tires you make squeal or their rubber burn,
No packages scattered or your drink you should spill,
Nor children or old folks to give them a big thrill.

But we do ask that you please notice our bad fate,
That behind you we're stuck and we just have to wait;
So please hurry around, complete the turn you plan,
Doing it safely, but as quickly as you can.

So let's check our new friends, they're out driving again,
Who's the worst of the bunch, it's hard to say will win.
Nervous Nell needs to turn, it's simply to the right,
Chatty Patty's behind unaware of Nell's plight.

Nell turned her signal on about two blocks ago,
Pat's given up on her, thinks Nell just must not know;
Suddenly Nell slows more and Pat's crowding her rear,
Nell creeps around the turn, Pat's tirade is severe.

Meanwhile, elsewhere, Ploddin' Paul's making a left turn,
Signal in his favor across he starts to churn;
Zack's headed toward him and decides to turn right,
No need to wait for green, Zack thinks he'll be alright.

Paul heads for the right lane, that's where he wants to be,
He knows there's a right turn in two more blocks or three;
Paul's right in front of Zack, who screeches to a halt,
With honking and swearing, he knows it's all Paul's fault.

Just a little thinking on any of their parts,
Would have saved wear and tear on many of their hearts;
In an empty vacuum none of us get to drive,
Helpful interaction might keep us all alive.

PS

If I had to admit my greatest driving fear,
It involves a right turn, that fits in well right here.
I see me turning right and to my left I check,
No on-coming traffic, my turn I start to trek.
Meanwhile, on the right side, someone decides to pass,
They've moved into my lane and given it the gas.
As my turn I complete I can suddenly see,
There they are dead ahead about to wipe out me.
We can always drive well and only slip up once,
And still wind up dead or sure feeling like a dunce;
So the more awareness that all of us possess,
Just might save some lives or eliminate some stress.

Driving For Dummies

Stop Lights or Signs

Driving discussions are mostly about going,
But about stopping there is more worth knowing;
"Things going up must come down," gravity does say,
And traffic in motion, will always stop some way.

There are traffic signals, lights that try to direct,
Our going and stopping, and all of us protect;
Knowing when it's our turn, if we should go or not,
Keeps all of us in sync and a bit less distraught.

So, Red means we should stop, and Green means we can go,
This we all understand, though some react too slow;
But it seems that Yellow is more misunderstood,
More confusion about reactions that we should.

Some want to hit the brake, get stopped soon as they can,
Afraid it will turn red before they cross the span;
Others more gas do give, always sure they'll succeed,
Getting across before we notice their bad deed.

What Yellow simply means is "Please take some caution,
We're getting ready to make the next transition.
The other direction we're about to release.
It's time to clear the intersection, if you please!"

Our proper reaction on traffic should depend,
For that's what will dictate how much time we can spend;
What's going on behind or happening ahead,
It's sure better to mesh than wind up being dead.

Sometimes there's no signal, it's only a stop sign,
Or the light is flashing, or out and just won't shine.
Then, an honor system we're supposed to follow,
Friendly interaction, so all of us can flow.

The system is simple, it isn't all that strange,
With cooperation, our turn it will arrange;
The first one that should go is the first to get there,
As alternating turns each direction does share.

We must patiently wait until the front we reach,
We can hope those ahead this plan did also teach;
At the intersection, we finally do get,
Our order remember and try not to forget.

It's easy to notice who was there before us,
Those are the next to go, soon as he or she does;
Then it becomes our turn, we are ready to cross,
It should go smooth enough, there isn't much time loss.

Now, while it sounds easy, there's frequent frustration,
Because there are those who add some complication;
Sometimes extra caution we do have to observe,
Problems to be resolved without rattling our nerve.

There often will be some who don't follow the rules,
Don't know if they have no honor or are just fools;
For these we just watch out, can't do much more than this,
And then just hope and pray we can help make them miss.

Sometimes a left turner extra tension can build,
They go with their side but for on-comers must yield;
Better if they move out and intent indicate,
Then make us all wonder, when they hold back and wait.

There are also those times when it just isn't clear,
Who got to the line first and should go without fear;
The rule that applies then, is the car on the right,
We let that driver go and avoid any fight.

When there's uncertainty and someone seems unsure,
You think they may have doubt and clarity prefer,
It's OK to give them a hand signal or sign,
Telling them it's their turn, which is perfectly fine.

Here we have our four friends at a stop light that's out,
Flashing red all four ways, there's confusion about;
Nervous Nell's turning left, and she's frozen with fear,
What the heck she's doing to others is unclear.

Ploddin' Paul's reached the front, going right toward her,
But whether Nell's going, he's completely unsure;
Meanwhile Zack and Patty, reach the front on each side,
They're both in a hurry, impatience they don't hide.

Already twice her side has gone without old Nell,
While she has just set there, nervous and scared as hell;
So Paul has waited some, thinking that she might go,
But now he's giving up, it's his turn he does know.

Patty has been chatting as the front she gets to,
A short pause that feels right and she just starts on through;
Zack didn't even pause, a gap he thinks he sees,
Right on through the whole works he thinks that he can breeze.

Right then, Nell finally decides to take her chance,
And she does venture out from her defensive stance;
They meet in the middle, all get there the same time,
And all cursing about the others' senseless crime.

Zack zips to the right and he uses the cross walk,
To get around old Paul, who for Nellie does balk;
Just in time, Pat does brake, as Nell crawls her way through,
They all miss each other, but angers they renew.

Well, as I am certain you can already guess,
Awareness and cooperation I will stress;
A little bit of time taken by each of them,
Would have gone a long ways to solving the problem.

Driving For Dummies

Miscellaneous

There are other matters we should also discuss,
Some more helpful guidelines that will help all of us;
There's not as much to say for separate sections,
So we will group these additional suggestions.

Emergency Vehicles

There are some vehicles to which we all should yield,
Those emergency ones, when on runs they are wheeled;
Police, Fire, Ambulance, with lights and sirens on,
We need to give them space until past us they've gone.

The goal again is their progress not to obstruct,
They can quickly respond and none of us are struck;
For them we should watch out, not them watching for us,
On the emergency it will let them focus.

Pull over to the side if you are where you can,
But don't forget others while making such a plan;
Sometimes it's best to just continue cautiously,
Rather than sudden acts, not made judiciously.

Concentrate on helping, this isn't about you,
Something more important they're needing to get to;
Others are in trouble, to whom this care must get,
So stay out of the way and don't cause them more fret.

Merging Traffic

Merging traffic is a common phenomenon,
So it would be great to know how it should be done;

By it's definition, merging always implies,
Sharing close time and space with lots and lots of guys.

With many vehicles in close proximity,
It's better if they're all near the same velocity;
So as you seek to merge their speed you need to reach,
That way you can fit in and no one has to screech.

When the merger gets there, to not be in a trap,
We need to cooperate and open up a gap;
Not cool to cut them off, it really is unkind,
How much diff'rence is ten feet ahead or behind?

When merging two full lanes the best way to get done,
Is working together each going one and one;
One from each lane and politely alternating,
It goes so much smoother when cooperating.

Lane reductions simply are mergers in reverse,
With speeds usually going down as we traverse;
The others' rates and positions if we respect,
We can all make it through and all of us protect.

There are always some who think that rules don't apply,
And they're going to try to zoom or squeeze on by;
Like a bully at school they'll push by you and me,
Just let them go, that asshole I don't want to be.

Working all together problems we'll minimize,
If mutual benefits we all recognize;
Better a few seconds to sometimes sacrifice,
Than hour long traffic jams to materialize.

Braking

It would seem that braking is just part of stopping,
But it seems everywhere we see brake lights popping;

Maybe a little time we should spend on it here,
So proper use of brakes is just a bit more clear.

Every car one drives has it's own certain feel,
And a bond with it you should eventually seal;
Steering wheel and gas pedal feel a certain way,
The better you know them the smoother you can stay.

The brake also has a very distinctive touch,
And one should quickly learn to give it just so much,
To stop just as quickly as circumstance dictates,
And not be too darn short or make excessive waits.

Braking's not just about how smooth that you can be,
Though that is important to passengers like me;
It also has effect on the drivers around,
Including just how quick your big rear end gets found.

Stopping short not only throws passengers about,
But it can also cause someone your rear to clout;
Your brake lights don't come on until the brake you hit,
Warning the car behind when they first become lit.

Riding the brake, that is, always on the pedal,
Is equally as bad, won't win you a medal;
Not only does it wear your brake equipment out,
It confuses traffic and fills us all with doubt.

Likewise, random braking for no apparent cause,
Can confuse all of us, leaving us at a loss;
We don't know what it is that you're doing in there,
And we can't tell whether all of us should beware.

Maybe you're just tapping some old song with your feet,
And you're catching the brake with that one certain beat;
If so, then leave it out, let it mess up your tune,
Better than causing wrecks, a lot more that will ruin.

Brakes are also signals, ways to communicate,
Not just that you're stopping, there's more you can relate;
Three short successive taps some danger would imply,
A warning to watch out, that a pass not to try.

The flash of your brake lights quickly gets attention,
So please make very sure that it's your intention;
And for the circumstance it should always make sense,
That way the rest of us can be on our defense.

Following

In traffic we can lead but we often follow,
Sometimes so close that it's difficult to swallow;
When traffic's packed so tight we see each other sweat,
It is always good to remember etiquette.

Following way too close, often called tail-gating,
On lots of drivers' nerves can be very grating;
And it is also true it can be dangerous,
If you can't stop in time it can be serious.

But dragging too far back is also upsetting,
When traffic has places they're working at getting;
And holding someone back can spark some quick anger,
Or invite cutting in which may bring some danger.

There are those that in car lengths try to calculate,
The proper distance back at which to operate;
When in heavy traffic it is better to track,
Half the distance between bumpers in front and back.

While you do watch in front for who you're getting near,
Don't forget who's behind approaching your own rear;
If you can't direct your attention where it begs,
You could be wearing your gas tank between your legs.

Starting up from a stop, someone you're following,
Try to keep up with them, no big gap allowing;
There are plenty of us also hoping to cross,
And if we're stuck behind, we'll be mad with our loss.

All in all, the best way to keep from getting hurt,
When in traffic make sure that you're always alert;
Instincts will even help to react the right way,
If you're at least aware that there's danger today.

Truckers

We should mention, too, our Big Buddies on the road,
Those drivers in big rigs hauling a heavy load;
To them these driving rules also mostly apply,
Though their situation differs from you and I.

The biggest difference between truckers and us,
Is that their size and weight, while making us nervous,
It slows down response time, how long for them to take,
Before a correction they are able to make.

As a result, we should cut them a little slack,
Don't mix it up with them, they pack a heavy whack;
Driving around them consider their weight and girth,
Making a change, try to give them a wider berth.

Longer to react and also to recover,
Another thing it'd help if we would discover;
It's nice if their progress we avoid disrupting,
Theirs' and others' schedules won't be interrupting.

It's not that they're owed special consideration,
But it doesn't take much to help good relation;
Making the old road just a bit happier place,
'Cause with our Big Buddies we often interface.

Handicapped

I might take a moment to acknowledge also,
When the handicapped sign is left in the window;
There are those that believe your vision 'twill impair,
But I know the reason that you've left it up there.

You're letting us all know that you can't drive well too,
And some extra caution we should take around you;
I appreciate that 'cause forewarned is forearmed,
We can be careful and not wind up getting harmed.

Not All-Inclusive

I'm sure there are plenty more topics to include,
Matters on which we could contemplate some and brood;
The intent is not to make sure we list them all,
But to hit the ones on which we most often fall.

Driving For Dummies

Exceptions

They say for every rule there is an exception,
And perhaps it depends on each one's perception;
To these rules we've covered, two exceptions I see,
And those we should explain, before finished we'll be.

The first one is a very real emergency,
Like where any delay could be a tragedy;
Maybe it's truly a matter of life or death,
Or baby on the way, 'bout to take it's first breath.

In these cases the circumstances justify,
Getting where you need to be fast as you can fly;
Try to be as cautious as you possibly can,
But getting there quickly is your primary plan.

If you can let us know, find a way us to warn,
Using flasher lights and loudly honking your horn,
Then we'll watch out for you and get out of your way,
Even though we'll wonder, or some choice words might say.

Please use enough caution you will get where you need,
Remember that quickness doesn't mean just more speed;
Your current condition don't further complicate,
With still more trouble that traffic can aggravate.

The other exception we should also discuss,
That often does effect very many of us;
Is bumper-to-bumper traffic in which we're stuck,
It's down to stop and go and we're just out of luck.

Maybe we caught rush hour at the very worst time,
Maybe an accident or some other dumb crime,
Maybe the game's over, everyone's headed out;
However it happened, we're stuck, ready to shout.

While the rules still apply, no choice really remains,
It's follow the leader, we don't have our own reins;
What the traffic allows is the name of the game,
We just follow along and it's sure not our blame.

Meshing with others is even more important,
'Cause margin for error is more non-existent;
Even the slightest change in rate or direction,
Can possibly have a big ramification.

So it's "don't rock the boat," "fit in best as you can,"
Try to hang in there 'til the mess it's course has ran;
Don't get too excited while the traffic's inert,
And try to do your best to keep yourself alert.

'Cause you don't want to be the one that in some way,
Winds up making a move causing extra delay;
Already bad enough, don't cause any more wait,
Or you'll be the target of lots of stares and hate.

In this situation, even though it is slow,
Along with the traffic you want to calmly flow;
Whether you'll be late is already decided,
You'll get there no quicker by getting excited.

One way to use the time is practicing excuse,
So you can explain away the time you did lose;
Or maybe make some calls, your schedule rearrange,
Maybe a better day to which you can still change.

And if all else does fail, you can do like I do,
Crank the radio up with good songs just for you;

Sing along, tap along, whatever that you would,
I drum my steering wheel, and I'm pretty darn good.

Driving For Dummies

Character Wrap-Up

What about our good friends we've used for example?
For bad driving mistakes they were very ample.
Are you curious some as to how they come out?
Fifteen years let's jump by to see what's came about.

After lots of close calls the two of them did ride,
Zippin' Zack and Patty finally did collide;
Pat was dazed and dented, but still texting away,
"OMG you should see this guy walking my way."

A whole stream of curses Zack was ready to shoot,
When he thought to himself, "Hey, this gal's kind of cute."
They did exchange numbers, and then started dating,
That led to a wedding, their marriage vows stating.

Zack's sports car got traded for a soccer mom van,
A few short years later when family began;
They had a little boy who they chose to call Fred,
That he'll be driving soon, both of them surely dread.

Meanwhile, Nervous Nellie went looking for a change,
She was tired of being scared and feeling strange;
She saw a therapist to treat her depression,
Which he helped her change to dynamic aggression.

She made it into the Police Academy,
She's the oldest graduate in their history;
Now she patrols the roads she used to fear so much,
And she keeps folks in line with a very firm touch.

Meanwhile, our old friend Paul just kept plodding along,
In spite of lots of honks he's sure he did no wrong;
Turns out he used to be one who did postal work,
And it might have gave him just a bit of a quirk.

One day Paul decided that he had had enough,
Dealing with the traffic had just become too rough;
He got himself a gun and he headed for town,
His worst intersection he would mow some folks down.

Before he got there he was pulled over by Nell,
And she informed him he wasn't driving so well;
There were plenty of words exchanged there on the road,
When suddenly somehow Paul's old car did explode.

Everybody thinks Paul died and met his judgment,
But he is alive and locked up in Nell's basement;
He doesn't mind so much, he gets three meals a day,
Watches lots of TV and in his bed can stay.

At times there are some things Nell does want him to do,
And while he's not for sure how he feels when they're through,
Even Nell's funny games and unusual tools,
Are better than driving and all those silly rules.

Driving For Dummies

Conclusion

An end we must reach at least eventually,
That's where we're headed now, you might think finally.
It was not my intent to accuse or berate,
But some common mistakes to simply illustrate.

I hope you got some laughs, or at least a few smiles,
Checking in on our friends and their driving trials;
I'm sure you could relate, you've seen plenty of these,
Seems like they're always there, each time we turn the keys.

But I do encourage in the mirror we look,
To see if we, ourselves, some small note should be took;
Could be that we could use a reminder or two,
I know that's true for me, maybe also for you.

While this piece I've written, I've noticed a bit more,
Paying attention to my own good driving score;
Going, stopping, turning, all with a bit more care,
Really just because I was being more aware.

Awareness is the first thing from drivers I ask,
As a critical part of the drive that they task;
Then simple courtesy, the other element,
Critical to a safe driving environment.

If we begin with awareness and courtesy,
A lot less challenges will confront you and me;
And those that do occur, more easily we'll solve,
If cooperation we're ready to involve.

For out there on the road our lives do intersect,
A quick, brief moment in time and space we connect;
Rather than curses and mad glares during that while,
I'd just as soon leave you with a nod and a smile.

www.danielspoems.com

Printed in Great Britain
by Amazon